Keyboard for t Absolute Beginner

Absolutely everything you need to know to start playing now!

Michael Rodman

Alfred, the leader in educational publishing,
and the National Keyboard Workshop,
one of America's leading contemporary music schools, have joined
forces to bring you the best, most progressive
educational tools possible. We hope you will enjoy
this book and encourage you to look for
other fine products from Alfred and the
National Keyboard Workshop.

ISBN 0-7390-2462-0 (Book)
ISBN 0-7390-2463-9 (Book and CD)
ISBN 0-7390-2684-4 (CD)

*This book was acquired, edited and produced
by Workshop Arts, Inc., the publishing arm of
the National Guitar Workshop.
Nathaniel Gunod, acquisitions and editor
Michael Rodman, editor
Gary Tomassetti, music typesetter
Timothy Phelps, interior design
CD recorded at Bar None Studios, Northford, CT*

*Cover photographs: Electronic keyboard courtesy of Korg USA, Inc.
Piano courtesy of Yamaha Corporation of America*

Table of Contents

About the Author

Michael Rodman is a composer, teacher, writer and editor from Allen Park, Michigan. He holds degrees in music from Eastern Michigan University and Bowling Green State University and is a doctoral candidate in music composition at the University of Michigan. Mr. Rodman has received numerous awards for his original music, which has been performed throughout the United States and Europe. He has also written on various musical topics for the *All Music Guide*, groovengine.com, *New Music Connoisseur* and other publications. A resident of Torrington, Connecticut, he is an editor at Workshop Arts, Inc.

● DEDICATION

To my parents and Clara Rogers, who led me through my years as an absolute beginner.

Introduction

Welcome to *Keyboard for the Absolute Beginner.* If you enjoy music and would like to be able to play the keyboard—but don't know where to begin—you've come to the right place. This book is designed to guide you through the fundamentals. You'll learn about pitches, note values, rhythms, using your hands and fingers, scales, keys and pedaling. You'll even find some tips for practicing. All the while, you'll actually be playing music—familiar folk tunes, well-known classical melodies and even some pieces with a rock and blues flavor. In this book, "keyboard" means nearly any keyboard instrument; you'll find that most of the exercises and pieces work well on piano, electronic keyboard, synthesizer and even organ. Music is an adventure unlike any other; learn as you enjoy, and enjoy as you learn!

There is a CD available for this book. Every example that is recorded on the CD is marked with this symbol. Track 1 includes an A 440 tone so that you can tune your electronic keyboard to the CD.

Track 1

Posture and Position

● Posture: How to Sit at the Keyboard

It's important that you're comfortable when you sit down to play. While you don't want to get *too* comfortable, the correct posture will give you maximum control and will prevent fatigue (or even injury) when you play. Here are a few rules of thumb (and fingers!) to keep in mind:

1. **Find a chair or bench that will allow you to sit at the proper height.** Rest your fingertips lightly on the keyboard as if you were about to play. Allow each hand to maintain its natural, gentle curve without forcing it or becoming rigid.

   Now, think of a line from the back of your hand to your wrist to your elbow. If you're sitting at the proper height in relation to the keyboard, this line should be fairly straight, and it should incline very slightly from your hand to your elbow. The idea is to find a position that will allow you to play with the greatest control and comfort. ————

Straight wrist

   Check to see if your seat is too high or too low.

   If the line from hand to wrist to elbow has a noticeably convex (arched upward) shape, your seat is probably too low. ————

Wrist convex, seat too low

   If the line has a noticeably concave (collapsed downward) shape, your seat is probably too high. ————

Wrist concave, seat too high

   It's never a good idea to play from a standing position; extreme bending of the wrists can lead to a painful injury. Some musicians, especially those in bands, often play portable keyboards from a standing position. In this case, the instrument should be raised to allow the proper position of the forearm, wrist and hand.

2. Sit upright with both feet flat on the floor. Your back shouldn't be straight as a board, but slouching and slumping will make it harder and more tiring to play. Use the front half of the seat, as opposed to sitting all the way back. This will allow you the greatest balance and flexibility of movement. Sit upright without tensing your back, and allow your feet to rest flat on the floor in front of you. One foot may be slightly ahead of the other. Plant your feet in such a way that you can bend slightly from the waist—forward, backward and side to side—without losing your balance.

Correct posture at the keyboard

● Position: Your Hands and Fingers

1. The natural curve of your hand is the best shape for playing. Make your hand into a claw shape, like you were about to scratch your fingernails down a blackboard. Then, with your palm facing the floor, splay your fingers out as far as they will go, like you were trying to pick up a basketball with one hand. *Now, never do these again!* These are the extremes to avoid when it comes to your hand position at the keyboard.

To find the ideal position, sit down and let your arms hang down freely at your sides. Let your arms remain in this completely relaxed position as you look at your hands. This gentle, natural curve of your palm and fingers is the perfect shape for your hand as you play.

Correct hand position

2. Use your fingers to best advantage. Most often, you'll play using the flat, fleshy part at the tip of each finger. Avoid flattening your hands or excessively curling your fingers so that the nails (rather than the flesh) are contacting the keys. By the way, trying to play the piano with excessively long fingernails is a little like trying to run in scuba flippers. Short, neatly maintained nails not only make it easier to keep your hands and fingers in the proper playing position, but also help you avoid that Morse code-like clicking that seems to haunt some pianists.

When you play, depress your fingers without slamming them down. Don't peck or poke at the keys. Instead, press down with a firm, steady motion until you feel the key hit bottom. If you feel yourself tensing up or getting sore, stop for a moment, shake out your hand and try again, remembering to allow your hand to assume its natural at-rest shape.

The Keyboard

Patterns make things easier, and the keys on a keyboard are laid out in a pattern that repeats over and over.

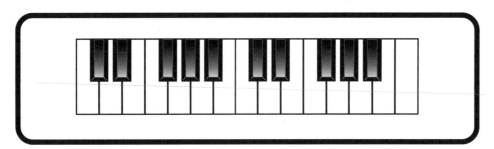

● Pitch

Just as this pattern of black and white keys repeats, so too does the pattern of pitches associated with these keys. A *pitch* is the specific highness or lowness of a musical sound. Musical pitches take their names from the first seven letters of the alphabet: A, B, C, D, E, F and G. Once you reach G, the pattern begins again at A:

A   B   C   D   E   F   G   A   B   C   D   E   F   G   A   and so on.

Each of these pitches corresponds to a white key on the keyboard. (Black key notes are just as important, but we'll discuss those later.) Here's how the pattern of notes is laid out:

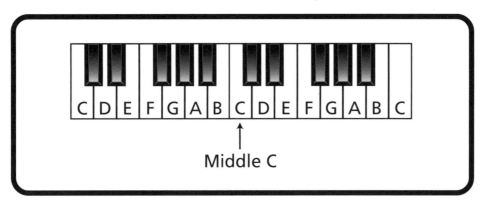

The C notes are always just to the left of a group of two black keys. The F notes are always to the left of a group of three black keys. The key marked "Middle C" is the C that lies approximately in the middle of the keyboard. It's important mainly as a point of reference; you'll often hear musicians refer to "the F above Middle C" or "the C below Middle C." It's helpful in much the same way as the "You Are Here" arrow on the map at the mall.

The Staff

Specific notes are indicated by their placement on a staff. A *staff* (plural: *staves*) is made up of five horizontal lines with four spaces in between.

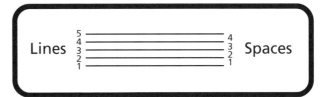

Each of these lines and spaces represents a pitch. Notes are written either directly on these lines or in the spaces.

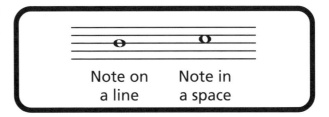

Each note takes its name from its line or space on the staff. The next section explains how the lines and spaces are named.

The Treble Clef

When you read keyboard music, the music for your right hand will most often appear in a staff with a *treble clef.* The treble clef is also known as the *G clef,* because the staff line that it curls around represents the note G. With this G as a point of reference, it's easy to find the rest of the notes on the treble staff.

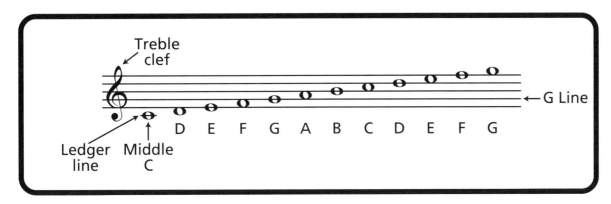

Notice that Middle C is shown on a short "extra" line called a *ledger line.* Ledger lines continue the musical alphabet above or below the staff.

One generations-old tradition among musicians is the use of certain words and phrases to remember the names of the lines and spaces in the staff. For the treble staff, the spaces are easy enough: from bottom to top, they spell out the word **F–A–C–E**. For the lines, **E–G–B–D–F**, one phrase that works well is "**E**very **G**ood **B**oy **D**oes **F**ine." You might even try making up one of your own: Each Goes By Darned Fast; Eggs Go Bad, Dear Friend; Eskimos Got Bob Dylan's Fish.

Fingerings

By showing you which fingers to use on which notes, fingerings help you to play in an efficient and musical way. *Fingerings* in piano music, which appear as the numbers 1 through 5, are usually written just above or below the notes. Each number corresponds to the same finger on both hands—1 is used for both thumbs, 2 for both index fingers, 3 for both middle fingers, 4 for both ring fingers and 5 for both pinkies.

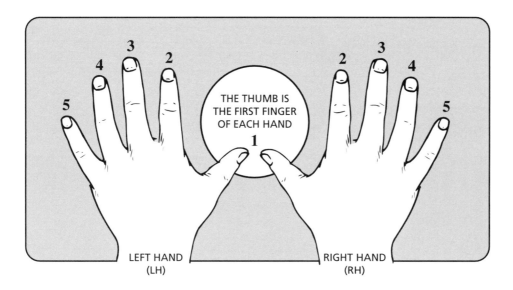

Sometimes, a single fingering here or there will make the fingering for the rest of a passage very clear. At other times, a piece of music may have no fingerings at all. In this book, you'll find fingerings for every example. When you begin to look at music that contains few or no fingerings, it's a good idea to write in at least a few to use as cues or reminders. As you become more experienced, you'll find yourself beginning to develop an instinct for fingerings that work well and feel comfortable. It all boils down to a simple principle: The better and more logical the fingerings in a piece, the easier it will be to play!

Composer and pianist **George Gershwin** *(1898–1937) bridged the worlds of popular and classical music with enduring works like* Rhapsody in Blue *(1924) and* An American in Paris *(1928). Many of Gershwin's performances at the keyboard survive in the form of player piano rolls, which have been made available on recordings.*

Tackle the Ivories: Treble Clef Exercises

Below are a few exercises to get you started reading and playing notes in the treble clef. The notes on the staff are *whole notes,* which we'll talk about soon. For now, just play the notes slowly and evenly, using the indicated fingerings. Release one note at the same instant that you play the next, maintaining a smooth, unbroken effect as you play. Each exercise is played with your hand in the same position, with the thumb on middle C. Try to play without looking at your hands. Let the notes and fingerings be your guide.

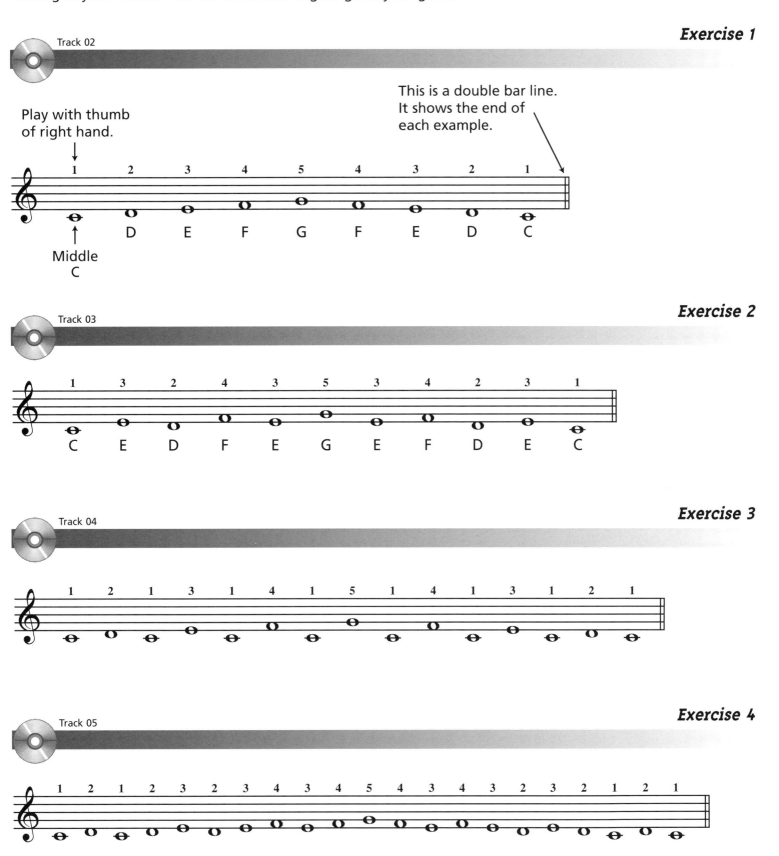

The Bass Clef 𝄢:

Just as the treble clef is most often associated with the right hand, music written in *bass clef* is usually played by the left hand. The bass clef is also called the *F clef,* because its hook and two dots show the location of the F line. All notes in the bass staff can be found in relation to this line.

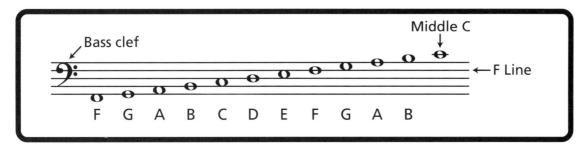

From the bottom up, the spaces of the bass staff are **A–C–E–G**. Try the phrase "**A**ll **C**ows **E**at **G**rass" as a memory aid. For the lines, **G–B–D–F–A,** remember that "**G**reat **B**ig **D**ogs **F**ight **A**nimals."

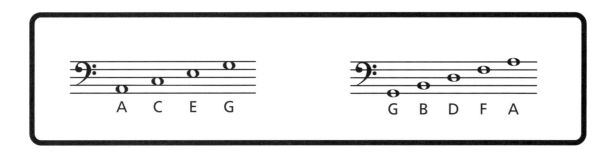

PHOTO • CHUCK PULIN/COURTESY OF STARFILE, INC.

Jerry Lee Lewis parlayed an exuberant stage presence and rip-roaring keyboard technique into a decades-long career as the "Killer." In 1989, Lewis rerecorded his greatest hits for Great Balls of Fire!, *a screen version of his rise to fame.*

● Tackle the Ivories: Bass Clef Exercises

The exercises on this page are similar to those on page 9, except you'll use your left hand and read from the bass staff. Play the whole notes slowly and evenly just as you did before, and try to create the same smooth effect with your playing by releasing one note at the same instant that you play the next.

similar to those on page 9

Exercise 5

Track 06

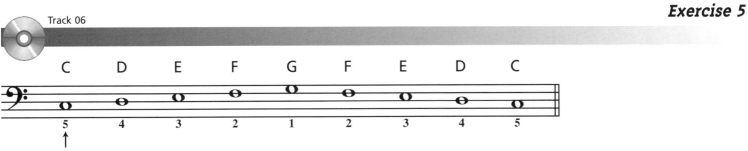

Play with 5th finger
of left hand on the C below middle C.

Exercise 6

Track 07

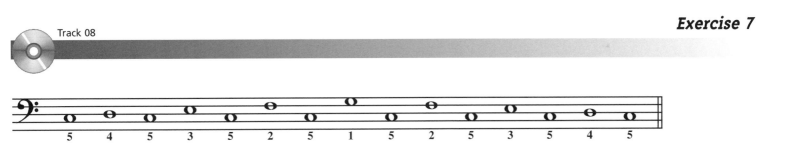

Exercise 7

Track 08

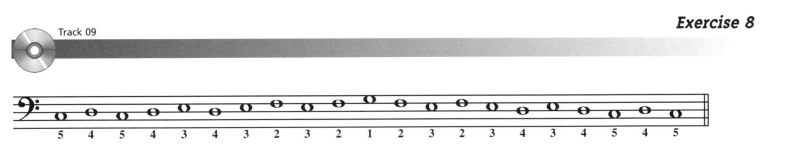

Exercise 8

Track 09

Rhythm and Note Values

Rhythm is the pattern of long and short sounds and silences in music. It's the fuel that keeps music on the move.

Rhythms are shown with note values. These *note values* show you the length of every note in relation to every other note. A *whole note* is the longest note value you'll usually encounter. It looks like this: —————

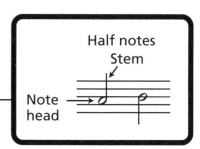

Whole note

The value of a whole note can be divided in a number of ways. For example, a note half as long as a whole note is called a *half note.* You can tell a half note by its oval *note head* and vertical *stem.* Notes on or above the middle line of the staff usually have stems that go down on the left. Notes below the middle line usually have stems that go up on the right. —————

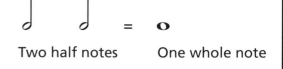

Half notes
Stem
Note head

Another way to look at it is that two half notes equal a whole note. —————

Two half notes   One whole note

A note half as long as a half note is a *quarter note.* The quarter note has the same stem as a half note, but the note head is filled in. —————

Quarter notes

Since a quarter note is half as long as a half note, there are two quarter notes in a half note, and four quarter notes in a whole note. —————

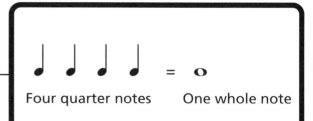

Four quarter notes   One whole note

It's possible to keep dividing notes into increasingly smaller values; for now, whole, half and quarter notes are all you'll need.

Beats, Measures and Time Signatures

Beats

If you've just run a marathon, stepped off a roller coaster, or spied the person of your dreams across the room, your heart is probably beating fast. If you're soaking in the tub, meditating, or watching a late-night infomercial for the tenth time, your heart is probably beating more slowly. *Beats*, equal divisions of musical time, are similar. If you ever tapped your foot as you listened to music, those were beats you were feeling—the steady, continuous pulse of the music.

Measures

Beats are organized into regular groups called *measures*, which are marked off by vertical *bar lines*. Sections of a piece are usually marked off by a *double bar line*. An entire piece usually ends with a *final bar line*.

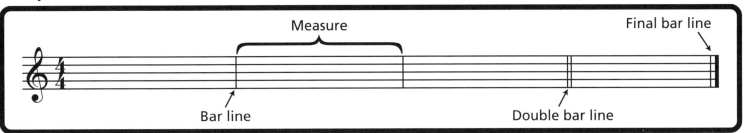

Time Signatures

A measure can contain any number of beats. This number is indicated by a *time signature*, which appears at the beginning of a piece of music. The top number of a time signature shows how many beats are in each measure. The bottom number shows which note value receives one beat ("4" indicates a quarter note). So, a measure of $\frac{4}{4}$ contains four beats, each equal to a quarter note.

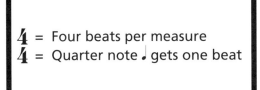

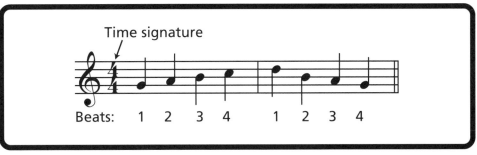

A measure of $\frac{3}{4}$ contains three beats, each equal to a quarter note.

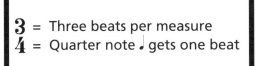

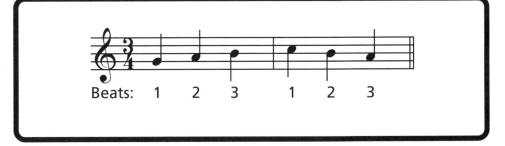

Tackle the Ivories: Rhythm and Time Signature Exercises

To get started using time signatures, you might find it helpful to write out the beat count under each measure, like this:

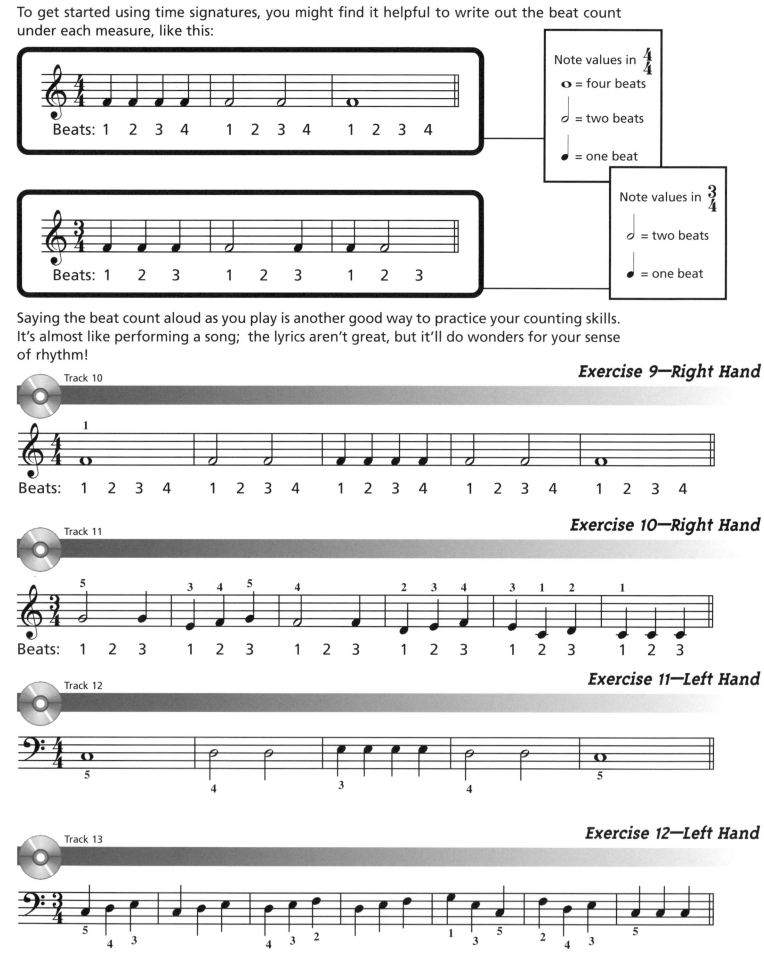

Note values in $\frac{4}{4}$

𝅝 = four beats

𝅗𝅥 = two beats

♩ = one beat

Note values in $\frac{3}{4}$

𝅗𝅥 = two beats

♩ = one beat

Beats: 1 2 3 4   1 2 3 4   1 2 3 4

Beats: 1 2 3   1 2 3   1 2 3

Saying the beat count aloud as you play is another good way to practice your counting skills. It's almost like performing a song; the lyrics aren't great, but it'll do wonders for your sense of rhythm!

Exercise 9—Right Hand

Track 10

Beats: 1 2 3 4   1 2 3 4   1 2 3 4   1 2 3 4   1 2 3 4

Exercise 10—Right Hand

Track 11

Beats: 1 2 3   1 2 3   1 2 3   1 2 3   1 2 3   1 2 3

Exercise 11—Left Hand

Track 12

Exercise 12—Left Hand

Track 13

Tackle the Ivories: Three Familiar Tunes

Now's your chance to play some familiar tunes. Play each tune slowly at first, making sure that the rhythms are accurate.

As you play these exercises, you may notice that the first four measures of each tune make up a kind of musical sentence, and the last four measures make up another. These four-measure groups each form a complete musical thought, called a *phrase*. Think of a phrase as a line in a song. As you play more and more, try to think in terms of creating phrases, rather than just playing a series of notes.

Track 14

Merrily We Roll Along

Track 15

Aura Lee

Track 16

Go Tell Aunt Rhody

The Grand Staff

Like typing, making a bed or eating corn on the cob, playing the piano is usually a job for two hands. Most keyboard music uses a *grand staff,* which is a combination of the treble and bass staves. One advantage of the grand staff is that it clearly shows the division of labor between the hands. Usually, the right hand plays the music on the treble staff, while the left hand plays from the bass staff. The grand staff is held together by a curly bracket at the left edge.

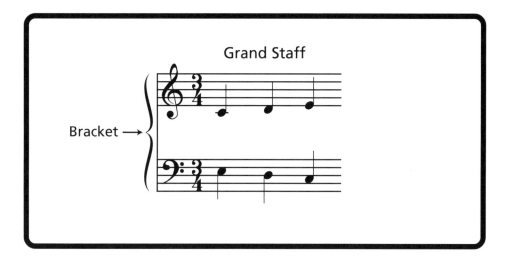

Divide and Conquer

While at first glance it may seem tricky to read from two staves at the same time, it's actually not so difficult. "Divide and conquer" is a good principle when it comes to learning music written on the grand staff. *Learn each hand separately before putting them together. Once you feel secure playing the hands separately, try combining them.*

Tackle the Ivories: *Two Pieces on the Grand Staff*

Here are two pieces that will help you get used to reading music on the grand staff. In the measures where one hand has nothing to do, you'll find a symbol called a *whole rest*, which looks like this: _____

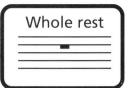

We'll talk more about the whole rest soon. For now, just think of it as a placeholder for measures that don't contain any notes.

Track 17

Back and Forth

M. R.

Notice that at the beginning of each measure, your right and left hands play together.

Track 18

Largo ("Going Home")

Antonin Dvořák
(1841–1904)

Together!

Rests

Music, like people, needs to rest every now and then. Sometimes, the feeling of "restfulness" in music occurs naturally. At other times, written-out *rests* are actually part of the rhythm, functioning like silent notes that punctuate a musical line. Think of rests as the sounds of silence!

Rests have values that correspond to the note values you already know.

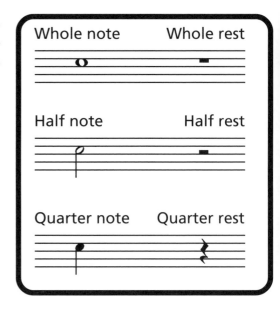

Notice that while half rests and whole rests look similar, half rests always sit on the middle line of the staff, while whole rests hang from the line above. As you've already seen, entire measures that are silent are marked with a whole rest, no matter what the time signature is.

The musical space rests take up is important. Be sure to always count rest values with the same precision you use for note values. In the middle of an active rhythmic line, or after a big buildup, rests can actually be quite dramatic. Don't steal their big moment by rushing through them!

● Tackle the Ivories: *Rest Exercises*

Play through these exercises to practice counting rests. Whenever you see a rest, simply release the key for the correct number of beats.

Exercise 13—Right Hand

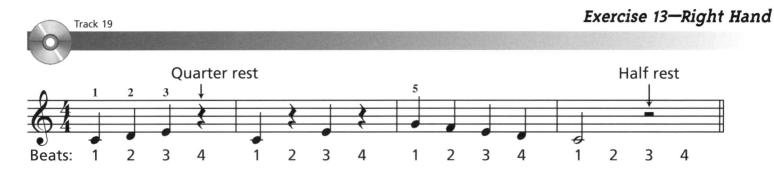

Exercise 14—Left Hand

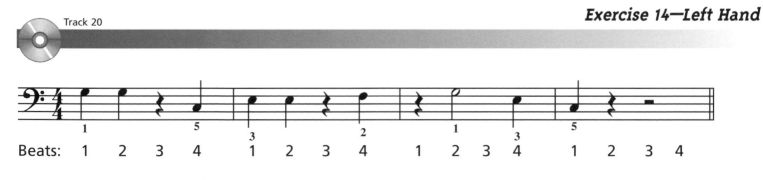

Tackle the Ivories: Pieces with Rests

Be sure to give the quarter and half rests their full value as you play *Restless Rests* and *Goodnight, Ladies*.

M. R.

Goodnight, Ladies includes some reaches and a change of hand position. We will start three white keys above the C above middle C. For reaches, simply extend your finger to play the note; there's no need to move your entire hand. There *is* a change of hand position in measure 5. Notice that you begin *Goodnight, Ladies* with the 5th finger of your right hand on E. In measure 5, you'll move your entire hand up slightly so that your 3rd finger is now on the same E that the 5th finger was playing. This is sometimes called a *substitution*. Your hand will remain in this position for the rest of the song.

Goodnight, Ladies

Traditional

Eighth Notes

You may have noticed a pattern in the note values you've used so far. Using a whole note as a starting point, successively shorter note values always decrease by the same proportion—that is, by half. For example, a half note has half the value of a whole note, a quarter note has half the value of a half note, and so on. Continuing this series, the next note value, which has half the value of a quarter note, is an *eighth note*. A single eighth note has the same head and stem as a quarter note, but also waves a *flag*. Notice that whether the stem is up or down, the flag is always on the right side.

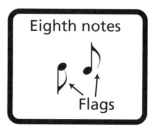

Groups of two or more eighth notes are usually connected with a heavy line called a *beam*. Beams actually provide quite a bit of information that makes music easier to read. In addition to making music look less cluttered on the page, beams clearly show rhythmic groups, and their slant will often tell you at a glance the general direction in which a group of notes is moving.

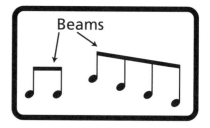

Like the note values you already know, the eighth note has a corresponding rest:

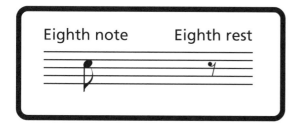

In $\frac{3}{4}$ and $\frac{4}{4}$, an eighth note is worth half a beat, so there are two eighth notes to a beat. When playing pieces with eighth notes, try counting as in the example below. Tap your foot as you count. On the numbered counts—1, 2, 3, 4—your foot will go down. On the "&" ("and") counts, your foot will come up.

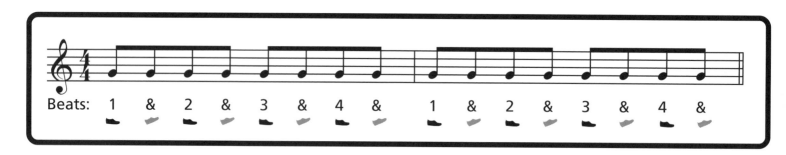

● Tackle the Ivories: *A Piece with Eighth Notes*

Long, Long Ago will give you some practice counting and playing eighth notes. The beat count is given for the first two measures; if you find it helpful, you might want to write in the counting for the rest of the piece. Notice the finger substitution in the first measure. This moves your hand up one position so that the 5th finger can play the A. In measure 7, fourth beat, use your 3rd finger on E to return to the original position.

Track 23

Long, Long Ago

Thomas Bayly

Ties

Sometimes in music, as in everyday life, there never seems to be enough time. What do you do, for example, if you're on the last beat of a $\frac{4}{4}$ measure, but want to put in that exact spot a note that lasts for *two* beats? How do you fit in that "extra" beat? Cram it into the end of the measure and hope for the best?

The solution is actually quite simple. A curved line called a *tie* (⌒ or ⌣) can be used to join the values of two notes of the same pitch. When a tie is used, the value of the second note is added to—that is, held over from—the value of the first note. Don't strike the second note, just hold it.

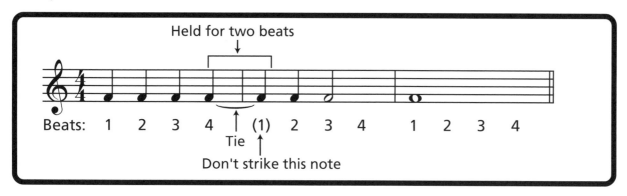

● Tackle the Ivories: *A Piece with Ties*

Track 24

Tied and True

M. R.

Dotted Half Notes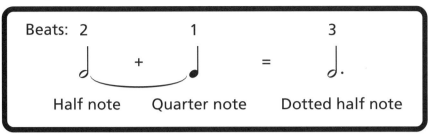

One way to increase a note's value is to tie it to another note. Another way is to *dot* it. By placing a dot to the right of any note head, you increase that note's value by one half. Dotting a half note, for example, is like tying a half note to a quarter note:

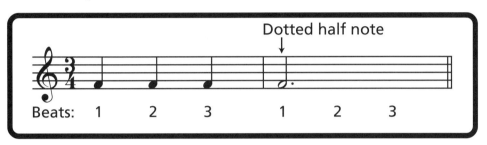

Dotted half notes are especially handy in $\frac{3}{4}$ time. Since a full measure of $\frac{3}{4}$ equals three beats, and since a dotted half note equals three quarter notes, a dotted half note equals a full measure in $\frac{3}{4}$.

● Tackle the Ivories: *Dotted Half Note Exercises*

Exercise 15

Track 25

Exercise 16

Track 26

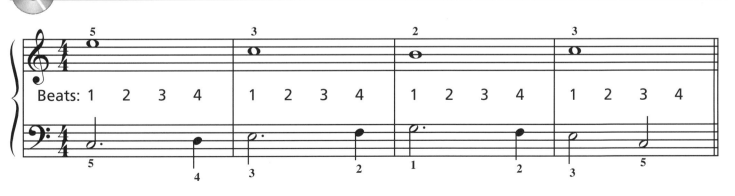

Dotted Quarter Notes ♩.

Dotted quarter notes work very much like dotted half notes. By placing a dot next to a quarter note, you increase its value by half—that is, by an eighth note. Dotting a quarter note is like tying a quarter note to an eighth note:

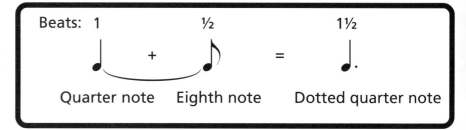

Dotted quarter notes are often followed by eighth notes.

⬤ Tackle the Ivories: *Dotted Quarter Note Exercises*

Track 27

Exercise 17

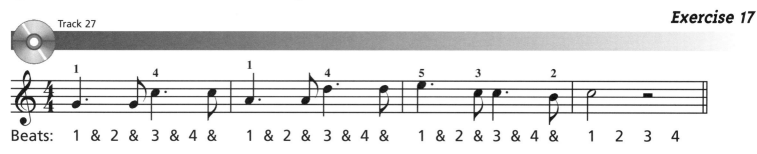

Track 28

Exercise 18

Track 29

Exercise 19

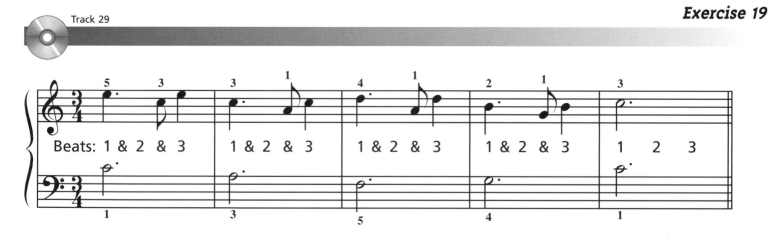

Tackle the Ivories: *A Piece with Dotted Notes*

Theme from Sonata in A Major includes dotted half notes in the left hand and dotted quarter notes in the right hand. Count the dotted quarter notes like this:

Beats: 1 & 2 & 3   1   2   3   1 & 2 & 3   1   2   3

Track 30

Theme from Sonata in A Major

Wolfgang Amadeus Mozart
(1756–1791)

This note is E

This note is D

Half Steps and Whole Steps

The distance between pitches can be measured in *steps*. The smallest distance between two pitches is a *half step*. On the keyboard, you'll find half steps between E and F and B and C.

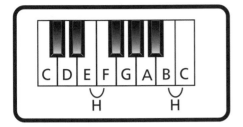

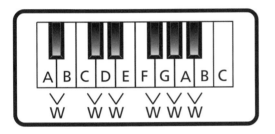

$\underset{H}{\smile}$ = Half step

A *whole step* is twice the distance of a half step. On the keyboard, you'll find whole steps between A and B, C and D, D and E, F and G, and G and A.

$\underset{W}{\vee}$ = Whole step

*In 1963, twelve-year-old **Stevie Wonder** (born Steveland Morris) made his first appearance on the charts with* Fingertips (Part Two). *From that point, Wonder matured into one of the most influential pop musicians of his generation, recording such hit albums as "Talking Book" (1972) and "Songs in the Key of Life" (1976).*

● Tackle the Ivories: *A Melody in Steps*

The melody of *Ode to Joy* moves almost entirely in half steps and whole steps. Notice that the rhythm includes both eighth notes and dotted quarter notes.

Track 31

Ode to Joy

Ludwig van Beethoven
(1770–1827)

Accidentals

Don't let any wisecracking musicians fool you into thinking that *accidentals* are mistakes, as in, "Guess I had a few accidentals back there when I was trying to play with my eyes closed." In fact, accidentals are handy symbols that tell you to raise or lower notes, or return them to their original pitch.

A *sharp* (♯) placed in front of a note raises the note by a half step. When this happens, "sharp" is added to the note name. For example, raising F by a half step changes the note's name to F-sharp (or F♯).

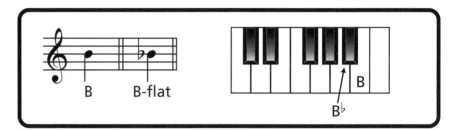

A *flat* (♭) placed in front of a note lowers the note by a half step. As with sharps, the note name changes, so that lowering B by a half step changes the note's name to B-flat (or B♭).

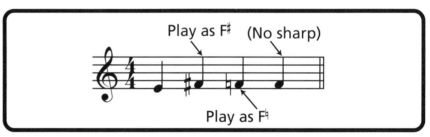

A third accidental, the *natural* (♮), functions as a sort of musical Terminator ("I'll be back")—it cancels out any sharps or flats previously applied to a note.

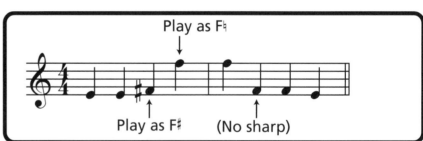

Accidentals apply to the entire measure, and only the actual line or space, in which they appear. Any accidentals that appear in a measure are cancelled by the bar line that ends that measure (and begins the next).

You may have noticed that some notes can be written in two different ways. Look at the black key between F and G on the keyboard; you could call it either F-sharp or G-flat, and both would be correct. Such "equivalent" notes are called *enharmonics*. Not all accidentals and enharmonics, by the way, involve black keys. Since there is no black key to the immediate right of B, for example, B-sharp is the enharmonic of C.

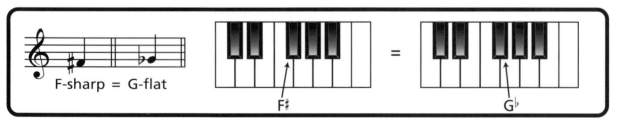

Tackle the Ivories: Accidentals in a Piece

All Through the Night includes both F♮ and F♯. Be sure to watch for the places where the sharp is cancelled by a bar line.

Track 32

All Through the Night

Traditional

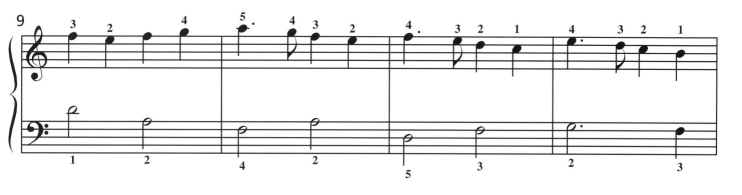

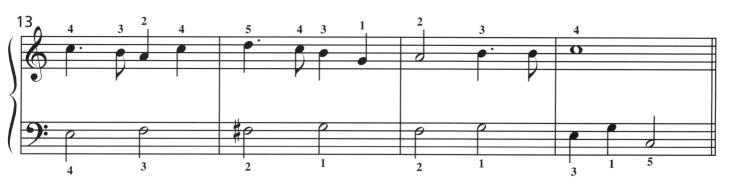

Major Scales

Just as one kind of step can be organized into a group called a staircase, steps in music can be organized in the same way. This musical staircase—the arrangement of a collection of pitches in stepwise order—is called a *scale.*

The unique identity of a scale lies both in the number of pitches in that scale and in the arrangement of whole steps and half steps between pitches. The workhorse among scales is the *major scale,* which is made up of eight notes in the following pattern of whole steps and half steps:

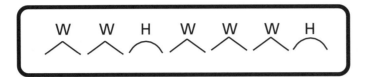

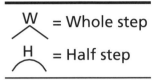

By following this pattern of whole steps and half steps, you can construct a major scale beginning on any note. The first note of a scale, called the *tonic* note, gives that particular scale its name. A major scale that begins on C, for example, is called the C Major scale; a major scale that begins on B♭ is called the B♭ Major scale. Notice that the last note of a major scale is the tonic, repeated an *octave* higher—that is, the next highest note with the same name. The specific position of each note in the major scale is called the *scale degree.* Scale degrees are assigned numbers, beginning with 1 on the tonic. The second note is scale degree 2, the third note is scale degree 3, and so on, up to scale degree 8 (the repeated tonic).

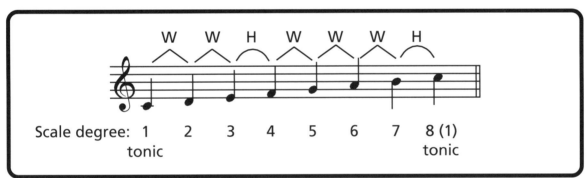

⬤ Tackle the Ivories: *Finger Crossing Exercise (Right Hand)*

Look at *Joy to the World* on page 31. Notice in measure 2 of the right hand that you go from C, played with your thumb, down to B♭, played with your 4th finger. This is an example of a *finger crossing.* To do this, simply lift your wrist slightly as you play the C, rotate your hand, still from the wrist, to the left, and reach over with your fourth finger to play the B♭. This next exercise will help you get used to the feel of finger crossings.

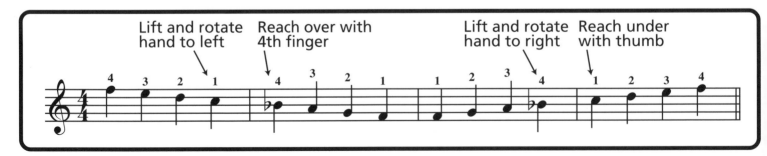

● Tackle the Ivories: *Finger Crossing in a Piece*

This arrangement of *Joy to the World* begins with a descending (downward-moving) F Major scale. Watch for the finger crossing in measure 2, and be sure to follow the fingerings; otherwise, you may run out of fingers!

Track 33

Joy to the World

George Frideric Handel

Keys and Key Signatures

Key

Imagine making a model of the solar system using pitches instead of painted styrofoam balls. In place of the sun, you'll use the tonic note of a particular scale. In place of the planets, you'll use the remaining pitches of the scale. This idea of a musical solar system, in which the tonic note of a scale serves as the center of gravity around which the other pitches orbit, sums up the function of a *key*.

Key Signature

The key signature is a group of sharps or flats that appears at the beginning of each staff. The pitches represented by these lines or spaces are always played sharped or flatted in every octave. For example, if the key signature contains a sharp on the F line, all the Fs in the piece are sharped. Only a natural sign can temporarily cancel the key signature. C Major contains no sharps or flats, so pieces in the key of C Major have no key signature.

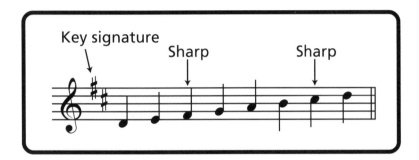

● Tackle the Ivories: *Finger Crossing Exercise (Left Hand)*

Alouette on page 33 contains two finger crossings. In the right hand of measure 6, you'll cross your 2nd finger over your thumb. This works just like the finger crossing you used on page 31. There's also a left-hand finger crossing in measure 8. Try the exercise below to get used to the feel of left-hand finger crossings.

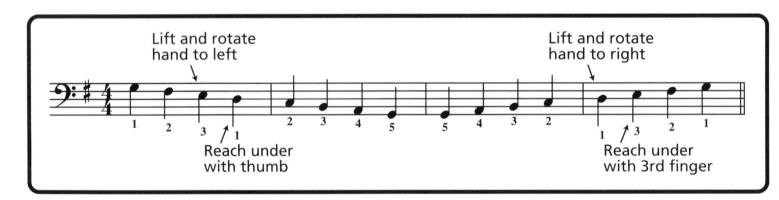

● Tackle the Ivories: *The Key of G Major*

This arrangement of *Alouette* has one sharp in the key signature (F♯), which means that you'll sharp every F you come across. This is the key signature for the key of G Major. The finger crossings you read about at the bottom of page 32 are marked in the music.

Track 34

Alouette

Traditional

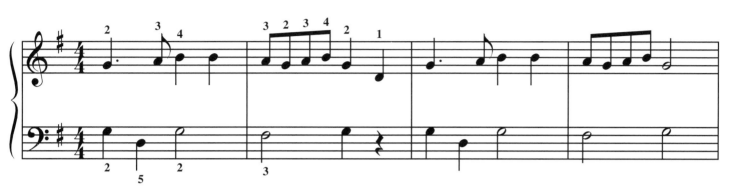

Finger crossing

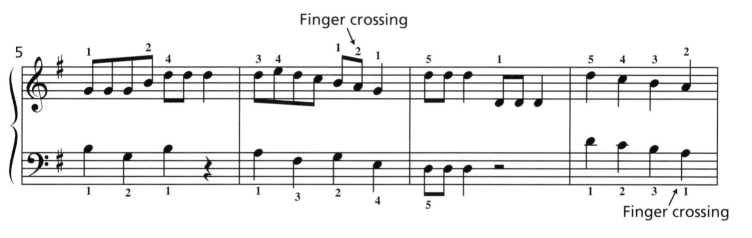

Finger crossing

Tackle the Ivories: *The Key of D Major*

This arrangement of *Camptown Races* has two sharps in the key signature, F♯ and C♯. This is the key of D Major.

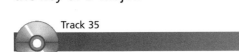

Track 35

Camptown Races

Stephen Foster
(1826–1864)

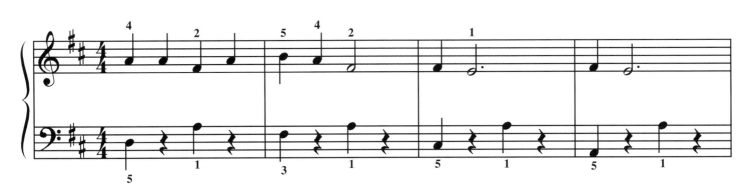

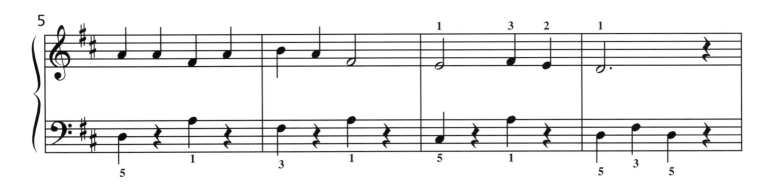

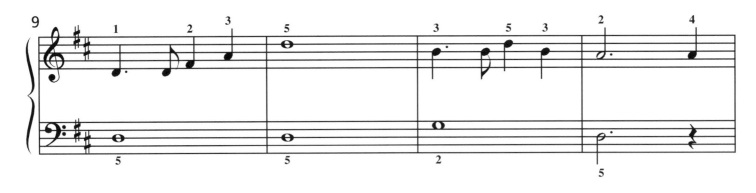

Pickup and Incomplete Measures

Pickups

While most music begins on the first beat of a measure (called the *downbeat*), it sometimes begins in the middle or near the end of a measure, almost like taking a breath before the first downbeat. This incomplete measure at the beginning of a piece is called a *pickup measure*, or just a *pickup. Home on the Range* is an example of a song that begins with a pickup. It's in ¾, but the first note falls on beat 3. Imagine (and count) silent beats on 1 and 2, then come in on beat 3.

Incomplete Measures

Pickups can range in length from a single note to a nearly complete measure. When a piece begins with a pickup, it ends with an *incomplete measure*. The incomplete measure is shortened by the number of beats in the pickup, so that the total number of beats in the pickup and the incomplete measures is equal to one full measure.

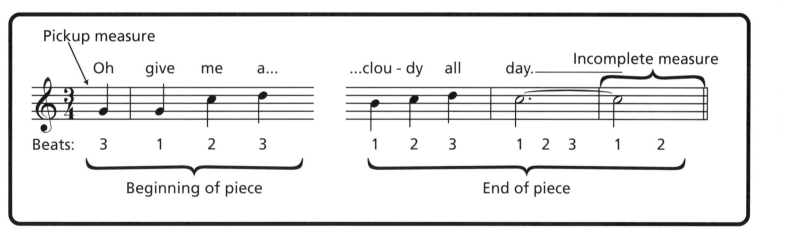

● Tackle the Ivories: A Pickup Piece

This famous theme, which is in $\frac{4}{4}$, has a pickup that begins on beat two. Notice that the final measure is an incomplete measure with only one beat. This incomplete measure, added to the three-beat pickup, makes a total of four beats—a complete measure.

Track 36

Finlandia

Edvard Grieg
(1843–1907)

Repeats and Endings

Repeats are the space savers of music. Sometimes, as in the different verses of a song, musical passages are repeated note for note. Instead of being written out repeatedly—adding pages and, even worse, page turns—such passages can be marked off with repeat signs, which do the same thing in a much easier way. Repeat signs look like this:

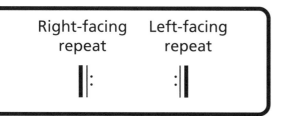

When you come to a right-facing repeat sign (that is, with the dots on the right), play on as you would normally. When you come to the left facing repeat sign, go back to the first one (the right-facing one) and continue on from there. It's that easy. In music that repeats from the very first measure of a piece, the right-facing repeat sign is usually omitted.

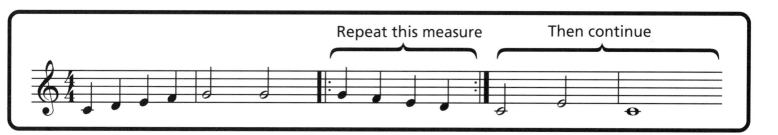

Repeat signs are often combined with other symbols that serve as a kind of road map. Repeats are sometimes followed by *first* and *second endings*. First and second endings work just the way they sound. The first time through, play the first ending (marked with a 1 and a bracket that shows you exactly which measures are involved); the second time through, skip the first ending and instead play the second ending (marked with a 2 and another bracket).

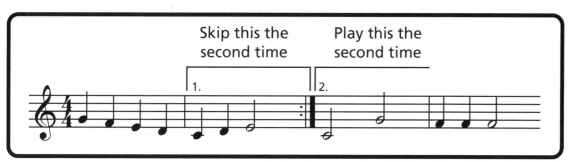

Tackle the Ivories: A Piece with Repeats

Blue Cheese uses a repeat as well as a first and second ending. When you come to the first ending, play to the repeat sign and go back to the beginning. The next time through, skip the first ending and play the second ending instead.

Track 37

Blue Cheese

M. R.

Tempos and Metronome Markings

Tempo

Tempo is like the musical equivalent of a speed limit. How fast you play a piece of music is often indicated by markings (usually in Italian, the traditional language of music) at the beginning. Here's a table of some of the most common tempo markings, from slowest to fastest:

Tempo Markings	
Largo	Very, very slow
Lento	Very slow
Adagio	Slow
Andante	"Walking" tempo
Moderato	Moderate
Allegretto	On the quick side
Allegro	Fast
Presto	Very fast
Prestissimo	As fast as possible
Ritardando (rit.)	Slowing down
Accelerando (accel.)	Speeding up

You can see how a single word can make all the difference in the character of a piece!

Metronome Markings

While the above indications are useful as a general guideline, one person's conception of *allegro* may be very different from someone else's. With the aid of an adjustable device called a *metronome,* however, you can find a particular tempo with great precision. There are several kinds, from the traditional windup type to electronic models that come with more extra gadgets than a Swiss Army knife.

Numbers on the metronome indicate the number of beats per minute. A setting of 40 will give you a very slow 40 ticks per minute, while a setting of 208 will give you a hang-on-for-dear-life 208 ticks per minute. Metronome markings usually consist of a note value (half, quarter, eighth, and so on) followed by the setting. For example, the marking ♩ = 100 tells you that each quarter note gets one tick at a setting of 100 ticks per minute.

Because metronomes don't fudge like musicians sometimes do—we're only human, after all—using the metronome during practice is an excellent way to ensure that you're maintaining a steady tempo. Try using a metronome while playing a tune you know; you'll be surprised by what a strict—but useful—taskmaster it is.

● Tackle the Ivories: *Tempos*

A *minuet* is a graceful dance, so play *Minuet* with a light touch, and don't hurry. The *Russian Folk Song* is more spirited. Practice it slowly until you feel comfortable with all the notes, then try playing it at a slightly faster tempo. Once you become comfortable with this new tempo, repeat the process to gradually build up speed. See if you can bring it up to allegro. Notice the key signatures. *Minuet* has one flat, B♭, which means that it's in the key of F Major. *Russian Folk Song* has one sharp, F♯, which means that it's in the key of G Major.

Track 38

Minuet

Leopold Mozart
(1719–1787)

Moderato

Finger crossing

Track 39

Russian Folk Song

Ludwig van Beethoven
(1770–1827)

Allegro

Dynamic Markings

Dynamic markings provide a road map for loudness and softness—and everything in between. By following dynamic markings, you and your fingers become the volume knob for your instrument.

Like tempo markings, dynamic markings (and their more common abbreviations) are usually derived from Italian. The next time someone puts on some music at a party, try shouting "Fortissimo!" instead of "Crank it up!" The following table shows the most common dynamic indications, from the softest to the loudest.

Dynamic Markings	
ppp (pianississimo)	= extremely soft
pp (pianissimo)	= very soft
p (piano)	= soft
mp (mezzo piano)	= medium soft
mf (mezzo forte)	= medium loud
f (forte)	= loud
ff (fortissimo)	= very loud
fff (fortississimo)	= extremely loud

Other markings allow you to control dynamics with even greater variety.

Crescendo (abbreviated "cresc.") means to gradually become louder. It's often indicated with a "hairpin" that opens to the right.

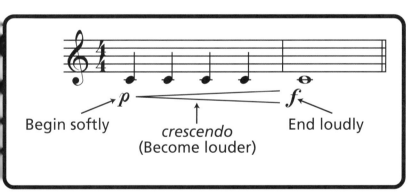

Begin softly   crescendo   End loudly
              (Become louder)

Decrescendo (abbreviated "decresc.") means to gradually become softer. It looks like the crescendo, except that the hairpin opens to the left.

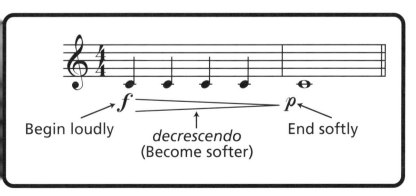

Begin loudly   decrescendo   End softly
              (Become softer)

Diminuendo (abbreviated "dim.") is essentially the same as decrescendo.

● Tackle the Ivories: *Dynamics*

As you might expect from a cradle song, *Lullaby* is meant to be played softly. Remember, you're trying to put a baby to sleep. Watch for the decrescendo in the last two measures. Notice the *rit.* indication in measure 15. This is short for *ritardando*, which means gradually slowing down.

Track 40

Lullaby

Johannes Brahms
(1833–1897)

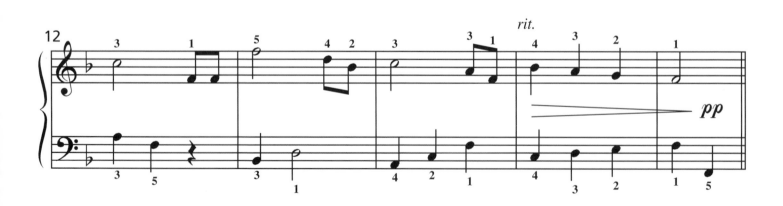

Articulations

Sometimes a note is just a note. But what if you want a note with some *character*? A brash, brassy note with attitude? A note that's the life of the party? The notes on a staff tell you *what* to play; *articulation* markings tell you *how* to play them. Articulations are what give a note or group of notes a distinctive voice.

Articulation Markings

∧	*Marcato*	Accented, stressed
>	*Accent*	Play the note a little louder
.	*Staccato*	Play the note short
−	*Tenuto*	Hold the note for its full value
⨪	*Mezzo staccato*	Play the note short, but not quite as short as staccato. Slightly detached.
⌒	*Fermata*	Hold the note longer than its normal value

Here's an example of what some articulation markings look like in printed music:

*Over the course of five decades, **Keith Jarrett** has moved with ease between the worlds of jazz and classical music. His exceptional talent as an improviser is evident in recordings that range from the famous "The Köln Concert" (1975) to the piano concerti of Mozart.*

● Tackle the Ivories: *Staccato*

Rockin' Staccato uses staccato notes, accents and a fermata. Play the staccato notes sharply—
not sharped!—but don't hammer at them. Watch out for accidentals.

Rockin' Staccato

M. R.

Using the Damper Pedal

Unlike the pedals in a car, the pedals on a piano (and some electronic keyboards) have nothing to do with starting, stopping or speeding up. Instead, they're tools for adding tone color to the music you play. Think of them as sonic paintbrushes—for your feet!

The pedal on the right, the one you'll use most often, is called the *damper pedal*. When the damper pedal on a piano is depressed, it lifts the *dampers* (which mute the strings when you release a key) off all the strings at the same time, allowing them to ring freely and producing a sustained, shimmering effect. The damper pedal on electronic keyboards usually produces a similar, but of course simulated, effect.

Markings for the damper pedal usually appear like this:

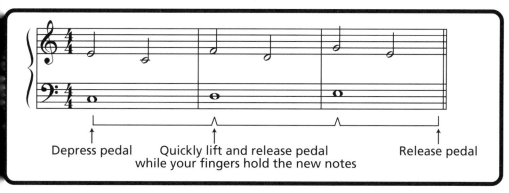

The use of the damper pedal is often left up to the player's discretion and taste. While all that resonance can sound very beautiful, it can quickly turn the music to mud. Be conscious of using the pedal; avoid using it where it really isn't needed, and don't use it as a substitute for smooth playing. Train your fingers to do most of the work!

◉ Tackle the Ivories: *Pedal Exercise*

Try this pedaling exercise, based on Pachelbel's famous *Canon in D.* Work on pedaling smoothly, without stomping and without letting the pedal snap up with a thud.

Track 42

From Pachelbel's Canon in D

Johann Pachelbel
(1653–1706)

Tackle the Ivories: *More Pedaling*

As you're learning *Andante,* be sure to practice the pedaling as well as the notes. Work on being able to depress and release the pedal in one smooth, quick motion.

Track 43

Andante

Ludwig van Beethoven
(1770–1827)

A Few Words about Practicing

Ask ten different piano teachers how much you should practice, and you'll probably get ten different answers. The amount of time that you practice is up to you—with the understanding that the more and *better* you practice, the faster and more solid your progress will be. Here are a few practice guidelines you may find helpful.

• Find a schedule that works for you—and stick to it!

Even if it's only 20 minutes or half an hour, a regular period of time that you devote to practice will be time well spent. Daily practice makes it easier to retain and build on what you've already learned, and by finding a time that is the same (or nearly so) every day, you'll develop a healthy habit. The trick is to find a block of time that you *know* will allow you to practice without interruption.

• Use your practice time wisely.

Have an idea of what you're going to work on before you sit down. Players are often tempted to spend practice time playing pieces they already know. The main idea of practice is to learn new things and fix old problems—not to present a recital. You might begin your practice session by warming up with a piece you can already play, but don't make this an open-ended amount of time. If you plan a half-hour-long practice session, spend, say, five or ten minutes—no more—playing pieces you already know, and move on. You can't play new music if you don't learn it first!

• Isolate, analyze and fix problem areas.

You're going to make mistakes as you practice. However, don't let mistakes go by without knowing what went wrong. When you make a mistake, take a moment to zero in on the problem. Did you misread a note? Use the wrong finger? Skip a page? Once you've figured out what went wrong, make the correction and play through the passage a few times. It's a good idea to begin playing a little before the problem area, and to continue a little past the area. That way, you know you'll be able to cover the seams of the problem area and be able to play it the next time without fumbling. Mark problem areas in the music so that you'll know to watch out for them next time. A sharp pencil is an indispensable piece of equipment for every pianist.

• Slow and steady learns the music.

As you're first learning a piece, it's important to take it slow so that you hear, see, and feel every detail—and learn to play the piece correctly the first time. If you find yourself making a lot of mistakes as you practice, it may be that you're not taking the time to learn which finger plays which note for how long at what point. Slow it down a bit, and give yourself and your fingers time to really learn the ins and outs of the music. Once you've become comfortable and can play without hesitation, then you can begin to speed it up. Frustration is your worst enemy. If things aren't going well, take a deep breath, get away from the piano for a few minutes, and come back refreshed and ready to go.

You've accomplished a lot so far, but you've only just begun. If you don't have a teacher yet, now's a good time to find one. There are hundreds of books out there for you to choose from as you continue your studies. Choose carefully, and look for something at the early intermediate level or lower.